NURSES

by Meg Gaertner

Cody Koala

An Imprint of Pop!

popbooksonline.com

abdopublishing.com

Published by Pop!, a division of ABDO, PO Box 398166, Minneapolis, Minnesota 55439. Copyright © 2019 by POP, LLC. International copyrights reserved in all countries. No part of this book may be reproduced in any form without written permission from the publisher. Pop!™ is a trademark and logo of POP, LLC.

Printed in the United States of America, North Mankato, Minnesota

042018
092018

THIS BOOK CONTAINS
RECYCLED MATERIALS

Distributed in paperback by North Star Editions, Inc.

Cover Photo: Shutterstock Images
Interior Photos: Shutterstock Images, 1, 9 (bottom right), 11, 12, 16 (right), 16 (left bottom), 16 (left bottom-middle), 16 (left top), 16 (left top-middle), 19, 20; iStockphoto, 5, 6, 9 (top), 9 (bottom left), 15

Editor: Charly Haley
Series Designer: Laura Mitchell

Library of Congress Control Number: 2017963079

Publisher's Cataloging-in-Publication Data

Names: Gaertner, Meg, author.

Title: Nurses / by Meg Gaertner.

Description: Minneapolis, Minnesota : Pop!, 2019. | Series: Community workers | Includes online resources and index.

Identifiers: ISBN 9781532160134 (lib.bdg.) | ISBN 9781635178081 (pbk) | ISBN 9781532161254 (ebook) |

Subjects: LCSH: Nurses--Juvenile literature. | Community health nursing--Juvenile literature. | Medical personnel--Juvenile literature. | Occupations--Careers--Jobs--Juvenile literature. | Community life--Juvenile literature.

Classification: DDC 610.7306--dc23

Hello! My name is

Cody Koala

Pop open this book and you'll find QR codes like this one, loaded with information, so you can learn even more!

Scan this code* and others like it while you read, or visit the website below to make this book pop.

popbooksonline.com/nurses

*Scanning QR codes requires a web-enabled smart device with a QR code reader app and a camera.

Table of Contents

Chapter 1

A Day in the Life

A **patient** comes to a clinic for a **checkup**. The nurse asks how the patient has been feeling. The nurse takes the patient's **vital signs**.

Watch a video here!

Vital signs include how fast the patient's heart is beating. They include how the patient is breathing. Vital signs tell the nurse about the patient's health.

Chapter 2

The Work

People who are sick or hurt usually see a nurse before they see a doctor. Nurses write down patients' health histories. They run tests to check patients' health.

Learn more here!

Nurses give patients medicine. They take care of patients' cuts and burns. Nurses help patients understand what they need to do to get better.

Nurses teach sick people how to become healthy. They also teach people how to not get sick.

Nurses often work many hours each day to take care of patients.

Chapter 3

Tools for Nurses

Nurses use many tools.

They use **stethoscopes** to

listen to a patient's breathing

and heartbeat.

Complete an activity here!

blood pressure monitor

syringe

stethoscope

bandages

clipboard

thermometer

uniform

Nurses use **syringes**, or small needles, to give people **vaccines**. Vaccines help people's bodies fight off **diseases**. Nurses poke the needle in a patient's body to give the vaccine. That is called getting a shot.

Chapter 4

Helping the Community

Nurses work with doctors. Some doctors know a lot about a certain part of the body. They might know a lot about the heart or the stomach.

Learn more here!

Nurses care for the patient's whole body. Nurses save lives and help patients feel better.

There are more nurses than doctors in the United States.

Making Connections

Text-to-Self

Have you ever been to the nurse? Would you ever want to be a nurse?

Text-to-Text

Have you read other books about community workers? How are their jobs different from a nurse's?

Text-to-World

Why do you think it is important to have nurses? What might the world be like without nurses?

Glossary

checkup – a set of tests to check a patient's health.

disease – a sickness or illness.

patient – a person receiving medical care.

stethoscope – a tool used by nurses or doctors to listen to a patient's heart and breathing.

syringe – a tool used to inject a vaccine or medication into a patient.

vaccine – something that doctors and nurses give to people to help their bodies fight off diseases.

vital signs – the most important signs that tell how healthy a person's body is.

Index

Online Resources

popbooksonline.com

Thanks for reading this Cody Koala book!

Scan this code* and others like it in this book, or visit the website below to make this book pop!

popbooksonline.com/nurses

*Scanning QR codes requires a web-enabled smart device with a QR code reader app and a camera.